Gardencycle™

A GARDENER'S DAY JOURNAL

SEEDS OF CHANGE™

EDITED BY
Howard-Yana Shapiro, Ph.D.

PHOTOGRAPHY BY
Scott Vlaun and Howard-Yana Shapiro, Ph.D.

TEN SPEED PRESS
BERKELEY, CALIFORNIA

Ten Speed Press
P.O. Box 7123
Berkeley, California 94707
www.tenspeed.com

Distributed in Australia by Simon and Schuster Australia, in Canada by Ten Speed Press Canada, in New Zealand by Tandem Press, in South Africa by Real Books, and in the United Kingdom and Europe by Airlift Books.

Cover and interior design by Toni Tajima, based on a design by Susan Caldwell.

First printing, 1999
Manufactured in China

1 2 3 4 5 6 7 8 9 10 — 03 02 01 00 99

GARDENCYCLE

AN INTRODUCTION

Henry David Thoreau wrote,

"FOR MANY YEARS I WAS SELF-APPOINTED
INSPECTOR OF SNOWSTORMS AND RAINSTORMS, AND
DID MY DUTY FAITHFULLY, THOUGH I NEVER
RECEIVED ONE CENT FOR IT."

Understanding the patterns and complex cycles of nature in our own backyards allows us to have insight into the larger structure of life that we are a part of. We can see our gardens as pieces of the puzzle that a gardener joins together through keen observation and planning. *Gardencycle* is an important part of this process. By providing a place for us to record the subtle changes in our gardens on a daily, weekly, or monthly basis, *Gardencycle* can help us organize our observations, making planning more effective. Few of us can clearly recall when exactly those changes in the weather occurred, when we planted our first seeds in a south-facing window, or when we, full of hope for the season, took our plants outside for transplanting. Recording these occurrences, along with highs and lows of temperature, the patterns of sun and overcast, wind conditions, and rainfall is an invaluable part of the encyclopedia of our gardens.

For eons the gardener has been this inspector. Recording such information year to year gives us a greater vision of the garden, one that goes beyond the plants themselves: it gives us a reflection of the traits and conditions that have been important for survival. Careful records show us about our gardens' adaptations—knowledge we can use to help our gardens adapt more successfully in the future.

We often forget, in the heat of summer or while weeding, that gardening is not solely about delicious fresh food for our meals or flowers for the table. Gardening is the connection we make to the cycles of life and to the plants, bugs, birds, and all that is around us. It's about the beauty of the various colors, shapes, and textures that we see daily, the fragrance in the early morning and late in the day. Gardening is our paradise here on earth.

Georgia O'Keeffe said,

"NOBODY SEES A FLOWER,
REALLY—IT IS SO SMALL—WE HAVEN'T
TIME, AND TO SEE TAKES TIME,
LIKE TO HAVE A FRIEND TAKES TIME."

Gardencycle is the place to take time for the garden—and for the gardener.

—THE STAFF OF SEEDS OF CHANGE

DAILY RECORD KEEPING

Any gardening expert will tell you that the main keys to gardening success are to keep good records and to use that information. Knowing nature's patterns and cycles helps develop a better understanding and respect that will assist every gardener in cultivating a more beautiful and abundant garden. Use *Gardencycle* to note your first and last frost dates, rainfall, planting, and harvest dates. Compile daily weather information using the data boxes that appear below each day on the calendar (see legend below). The data boxes help you keep track of high and low temperatures, wind speed and direction, precipitation, and general weather conditions. This type of data can be crucial for identifying weather trends and maximizing results in the garden.

THE WEEK-BY-WEEK CALENDAR

To use the book, simply write in the dates at the top of each weekly calendar spread, beginning with the first Monday of the year. For example, the first Monday in 2000 falls on January 3. At the top of the first *Gardencycle* calendar spread, you would write: "Week of January 3 to January 9." The following calendar spread would be labeled "Week of January 10 to January 16," and so on. If you wish, you can also label each day of the week with the proper date.

MONTHLY GARDENING NOTES

Throughout *Gardencycle* you will find space for recording gardening notes for each month. The notes pages are located at the beginning of each season—one every three months—with space provided for each month in the season. At the beginning of the Winter section of the calendar, for instance, you

will find space for January, February, and March. Use these pages to record observations about your garden's design and productivity, unusual weather patterns, ideas for improving next year's garden, seed company addresses, or any other useful information.

SEASONAL GARDEN PLANNING

Nature does not observe the months of the year; instead, it follows seasonal patterns. That is why we have chosen to organize *Gardencycle* by season instead of by month. Use the Seasonal Garden Planning pages located at the beginning of each season section to outline gardening goals, sketch garden designs, or list an overview of seasonal tasks. Thinking seasonally helps us stay attuned to our garden's natural cycles.

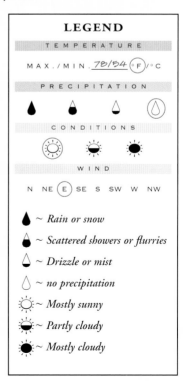

LEGEND

TEMPERATURE

MAX./MIN. _78/54_ (F)/°C

PRECIPITATION

CONDITIONS

WIND

N NE (E) SE S SW W NW

⬛ ~ *Rain or snow*

◮ ~ *Scattered showers or flurries*

△ ~ *Drizzle or mist*

◇ ~ *no precipitation*

☀ ~ *Mostly sunny*

◓ ~ *Partly cloudy*

● ~ *Mostly cloudy*

HOW A GARDEN

I have lived for many years in a small American village, but I am not a native. I grew up in another country, and when I first moved, there was confusion about words. One spring morning, with the grass just greening up nicely and the daffodils yellow, I was hanging the washing on the line when the man next door called over the fence to ask if I was going to put in a garden this year. What could he mean? I wondered. I was *in* the garden; surely he could see?

In time I discovered that in and around my village the "garden" was the plot, tilled each year, where vegetables were grown, and maybe some zinnias to cut. The space around that plot was the "yard." When my children were born, I made an effort to speak the language of their native place to make them feel at home. But I drew the line at the New England restraint of "yard." I would not send them to play in the yard; it was important that they be "in the garden." I felt this phrase to be enchanting, although at first, this had nothing to do with anything we could see.

When our family grew and we bought a house of our own, we bought it for the garden—or what I thought was the garden. I saw it first under January snow, unfolding its way under high-branching trees in a gentle eastward slope down to reeds, a tidal pond, and in the distance, the glint of the sea under a white sky. That the house squatted by the road, behind a dusty screened porch and windows hooded with heavy aluminum shades, was

immaterial. I would only wait for warm weather to come and bring the garden to life.

Spring came, but the garden did not wake up. A little grass grew but quickly browned, the trees leafed out too high for us to smell or touch their leaves, and the earth, when I dug in my spade, was gray and moribund. The place had the feel of a desolate parking lot, which we soon discovered was not far from the truth. There was no driveway or fence, and cars and oil trucks, apparently from long habit, often pulled in higgledy-piggledy anywhere—the cause, no doubt, of the compacted, cementlike soil.

Though we had taken down the house's aluminum eyelids and impenetrable screens, the fact they had existed—that not one window had simply looked out—suddenly took on significance. When the people who live beside it avert their gaze, there can be no garden. If there was to be a garden, we ourselves would have to bring it to life.

So we began. Because the children were small, the first necessity was keeping out the cars. Leaving only the smallest space for parking, we paced out a line on the ground and built an unmistakable fence. No more tires would gouge the earth, and children could safely play. Everything inside the fence, bleak though it still was, shimmered with possibility.

Next, because the lifeless soil required radical measures, we borrowed a small young calf from a farmer friend and allowed her to wander about on a long tether, happily grazing the summer's grass. We hoarded her droppings to layer with that autumn's leaves and make a rich compost. Long after the calf was returned to the farm, I felt how her gentle footsteps had enlivened much more than the soil.

That first autumn, our oldest child and I went

CAME TO LIFE

CAROL WILLIAMS

to work planting bulbs (which carry their own nourishment): daffodils, fritillaries, crocuses, hyacinths, and snowdrops. So the second spring was filled with flowers, and every bloom drew an attentive bee or tiny wasp. The sweetness of the upturned petals opening in the sun reminded me of the little calf and made the baby smile.

Serious cultivation had to be postponed. There were too many trees and not enough sunlight. At least one great tree would have to go. It took a year for us to decide which one. (Where would its absence let in the most light? Which was past its prime?) Then we cut it down and made a woodpile. Now we could position the first beds: long ones against walls for columbines, roses, anemones, and flax—the vocabulary of flowers I was only beginning to learn. We planted shorter beds, reachable from all sides and out in the fullest sun, for chard, spinach, leeks, and potatoes. Circular ones let the roots of apple and pear whips find their way unobstructed.

We double-dug and composted, sprayed biodynamic preparations, and planted. Some of what we planted thrived, and some did not; this was chiefly how I learned. And matters did not always stay in bounds. The grasses, now green and vigorous, continually ran into the beds while the violets ran out to the grass. Oriental poppies opened next to spinach, and a turtle climbed out of the pond to lay eggs in a hole in the lawn.

I cannot say we ever had a plan. Instead, year by year and day by day, we did what the garden seemed to ask. Nor can I say that, even after twenty years, we ever brought the garden to gracious maturity. There were moments when it took our breath away with radiant abundance and others when it

threatened to return to lifelessness. Hurricanes felled huge trees and washed compost piles out to sea. Worse, family storms turned our eyes away, causing things to begin once again to die. At such bad times, the ravaging deer came in, and one early morning I stepped into the garden to meet the eyes of a giant stag, his antlered head thrown back as he ripped strip after strip of bark off the pear tree.

With the help of friends, half the garden is now fenced in, and half is now a wild place, mowed twice a year, for the deer, foxes, and tides. This year the pear tree bent its branches all the way to the ground with the weight of so much fruit. Eventually the oldest child, the one who planted bulbs, left home and traveled around the world.

At length he came back to visit; I picked him up at the station late at night. In the morning while he slept, I went out to the garden to pick some flowers for the house. It was one of those in-between moments when not much is in bloom, so I had to search every corner. In the end I found some harebells, a little ragged phlox, a sprig of sea lavender, and a small pale rose, and put their thin stems in a jam jar on the kitchen table.

Over breakfast the traveler told stories of Budapest and Prague, of sleeping in Alpine meadows, crossing a war zone, looking down at the Aegean from a high white village. After an hour he paused and stretched, focused his eyes on the jar, and said, "Those are the most beautiful flowers I have ever seen."

THE CHILDREN'S

From September through June the garden at the French-American School in Berkeley, California, is a work in progress. As nature plays out its seasonal cycles, the students from kindergarten through third grade assume the role of caretakers—continuously adding to their garden, maintaining it, and exploring its bounty.

When the students return from summer break in early September, they find their garden has been as active as they, flourishing in the long summer days. The students who have shared in the garden's life for the past three years return with expectations of verdant abundance. They anticipate the towering sunflowers, with massive heads so weighted with seed centers that they bend heavily towards the ground, gesturing like welcoming giants to their returning caretakers. The students run to their garden beds to find tomatoes of various shapes, colors, and stages of ripening; mammoth zucchinis lolling heavily on the soil's surface; beans by now the size of a grown-up's fingers; and the brilliant nasturtiums in grand clusters, their yellow and orange heads jutting from their delicate, determined stems. The "ooohs" and "aaahs" of delight intensify as eyes jump from plant to plant, and hands eagerly reach to touch "my tomato plant" and "my flowers."

Months before, in the cool dampness of early spring, these little hands—now noticeably bigger—had begun to prepare the beds' soil with compost and to choose as a group which vegetables and flowers to plant. The comments were lively:

from, "I want to grow little yellow tomatoes—they're juicy!" to, "Not zucchini, it's yucky!"

Once the choices were made, the seeds were planted—busy hands sticking fingers in the dirt to just the right depth, seeds dropped in, and the soil patted over. Some of the seeds had already been started in egg cartons, and the seedlings were transplanted into the garden beds. In the weeks ahead, there would be chores for all—watering, pulling weeds, and ridding the garden of the uninvited critters. During their weekly visits to the garden, the students laughed, played, and experienced the freedom of spending time in an atmosphere much different from the classroom. In the garden the rules are eased. Work feels like play, and talk is free flowing.

As the garden began to come alive, the students celebrated with their first "official" tasting—lettuce. They made vinegars with herbs and garlic, and they picked the flowers and blossoms of borage, pansies, and zucchinis, discovering that they are delicacies to the palate as well as to the eye. The seeds of the sunflowers were plucked in the fall and devoured, along with the annual tomato tasting. Autumn also brings the Harvest Festival, where the garden booth is one of the most active attractions—a success in terms of pride as well as money raised for seeds and garden supplies.

Now, on a cold, wet day in January, a group of student gardeners, Ethel Brennan (the school gardening teacher), and I sit huddled around the picnic table in the garden to talk about what the school garden means to the kids. I look around at the beds and think what a different sight it is from a few months ago. The plants are lower and there's little color, except for a few single crocuses, young fava

GARDEN

LAUREN WEBB

With special thanks to Ethel Brennan and all the enthusiastic student gardeners at the French-American School.

bean stalks, and clusters of red chard. As we approach Class 22's garden bed, hands immediately come out of pockets to feel the lamb's lettuce, and the students discuss what they've learned about seasonal planting and which plants grow well in winter.

We also talk about root vegetables and what's going on under the soil. They ask Ethel, "Are the radishes and carrots ready?" Ethel replies, "Let's check." Hands go to the stems, and heads move in close to see if there are any signs on the surface. A gentle pull reveals small but developed red and orange spindles. As the clinging dirt is brushed off and the delicate radishes and carrots are tasted, discussions run in all directions. Eventually, though pleased with nature's gifts, the children decide that the vegetables need more time.

Ethel presents a question to the group that changes the mood of the discussion, stretching each young mind to an unpleasant thought: "How would you feel if, when you came to school tomorrow, the garden was gone, and the head mistress and class teachers decided not to have a garden anymore? What would you tell them?"

Hands go up and voices start to speak, "I'd feel lonely if the garden was gone," says the first voice. It continues, "The plants are like my friends, and I like taking care of them. I like the responsibility."

"Yeah, it teaches you to take care of things, and you can see if you take care of something and come back, it's still alive."

"Plants give back if you take good care of them. It makes me feel proud."

The flurry of thoughts and emotions continues: "I would feel sad—it feels good to help the plants."

"If we didn't have the garden, we wouldn't have learned that seeds make plants, and they have seeds, and they make more plants."

"I like the bugs and animals."

"On garden day I feel good. I'm excited that I'm going to be able to taste the vegetables that we're growing."

"We love the garden, and we love the stuff in the garden . . . the salad. We learn how to plant the seeds and how deep. We learn to eat good food."

"I wouldn't be able to taste the strawberries . . ."

As I stand among this group of young gardeners, as we talk, taste, and listen, what comes to mind is the "thread of ritual" and the expression of the heart. It is a ritual that has gone on for generations between young and old, farmers and neighbors, seed savers and friends, parents and children, and here between a class of students and their gardening teacher. I realize how sacred this place is to these children. I'm struck by their sense of caring for life and by their enthusiasm for nurturing and maintaining the garden. They have expressed so profoundly their understanding of the seasons and the importance of nature's cycles—an understanding they have gained from spending time in the garden. These young gardeners will apply and build on these experiences and knowledge through their lives, along with the sense of connection and pride that they hold in their hearts.

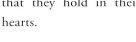

R O D A L E

BY ANTHONY RODALE

Robert Rodale, the son of J.I. Rodale, founder of the organic movement in the United States, grew up in a very exciting time. The organic pioneers worldwide were developing an idea they never knew would have such an impact on the world today.

In the United States especially, J.I. and Bob Rodale were key leaders in this pioneering group, helping to design the blueprint for today's burgeoning organic food acceptance and market expansion. They were able to persevere and succeed during these challenging years because they found strength in each other—strength came from an understanding, love, and respect for the soil and for nature itself. In memory of his father, my father wrote, "I will always remember J.I. Rodale not only as my father, but as a man who taught me to think of myself as an organic person, trying to live in nature, striving always to improve the environment while working to improve myself, too. That was the message to me, and it will live on for a long time."

This philosophy was developed from the practical experience of working with the soil. My father lived on the original Organic Gardening Experimental Farm in Emmaus, Pennsylvania. His father, J.I., designed this diversified farm with the primary goal of growing enough organic food to feed his family. A secondary goal was to conduct experiments that would help evolve and define organic gardening and farming techniques. And finally, J.I. wanted the farm to be a place where people of all ages could come and learn firsthand about the principles of gardening and farming organically.

But perhaps even more importantly, the original Organic Gardening Experimental Farm was the perfect training ground for what my father was to become: the world's greatest organic journalist. That farm experience—living, working, and personally experiencing the connection between soil, human, and environmental health—was the first of four stages in my father's life that helped him develop his insight into the world around him. Through all of these stages, practical experience—whether making and applying compost on the farm or writing about the people he actually visited and learned from—would remain the foundation of his work and vision.

That was especially true in the second stage of his life, when he began to put that practical farm experience to work by writing for *Organic Gardening & Farming* magazine. Developing *Organic Gardening & Farming* and *Prevention* magazines in partnership with his father, reaching people worldwide through his monthly articles, was one of his most important achievements. Always in search of new ideas and understandings, he followed J.I.'s

advice: "If you really want to understand a subject of interest, start a magazine." But this on-the-job training wasn't enough. Wanting to know more, my father, as a young man, drove by himself across the United States and down to Mexico, visiting farms and gardens along the way. It was an experience that would help open his eyes further into the world and impact his approach to writing for the rest of his life. When he reached Mexico, he was especially fascinated by the people, their culture, and the land. He saw the challenges people faced growing food, but he also realized that the people were happy. To these people and to my father, growing food was not a hobby, as most Americans look at it. It was a matter of survival. Although it contrasted with his early upbringing in an urban environment, my father viewed growing food as a way of life.

This international experience in Mexico also helped strengthen my father's talent for writing about gardening and farming. It also taught him the importance of sharing information and experiences about what others were doing around the world to try to improve their quality of life.

My father worked with J.I. for about 20 years as a cutting-edge writing and publishing duo, expanding the organic concept and gaining widespread national attention for their ideas. Then tragedy struck with J.I.'s unexpected death in 1971. Despite the difficulty of my grandfather's death, my father

was ready to continue on his own. He had reached the third stage of his life, and he now had the grounding and practical experience to evolve the organic concept to a new level—the development of his favorite concept: regenerative agriculture with a global approach.

Deeply ingrained in him by now was the idea that he was "thinking as an organic person, trying to live in tune with nature, and always striving to help improve the environment while working to improve oneself." That was the right foundation for my father to take the organic concept beyond its perceived image of the 1960s and '70s. Building on his trip to Mexico, where he realized that growing food was about health and survival and not about an alternative lifestyle, he was ready to answer a growing list of critics. "Prove it," the scientists and agri-business professionals said. "Show us organic farming can work on a large scale." He accepted the challenge. And with that came the birth of the new Organic Experimental Farm, which today is home to The Rodale Institute.

As the new organic research trials were put into place, my father never stopped traveling the world to learn how people were growing food. And he didn't stop talking and writing about what he was learning from farmers and gardeners. The pace at which he traveled and wrote reached an almost consuming intensity, which was not surprising to those who knew him well. He was highly competitive in many areas. (Not too many people knew, for instance, that he was a world-class skeet shooter.) He used his competitive energy to define the science of growing foods organically, profitably, and in tune with nature. He often said, "When people tell me it can't be done, that's when my juices begin to flow."

It was through his intimate, personal involvement with the soil and the research program of the "new farm," as he called it, that he came to realize that there was a new level to organic farming. That new level was about the relationship one has with the land—integrating the needs of both the individual and the land itself. To get what we need from the soil, we have to give the soil what *it* needs: we must help it replenish itself to build its fertility. Over

those early years, he saw the land almost literally regenerating itself before his eyes.

This is how the concept of regenerative food production was born. Using his global journalism skills, my father wrote about regenerative gardening and farming in his monthly *Prevention* and *Organic Gardening* articles. His attitude shifted from thinking as an organic person to thinking as a regenerative person. And in the process, my father's travels, thinking, and writing began to move him beyond the garden and farm. He theorized that if nature can regenerate itself, maybe with the right attitude, people can regenerate themselves and their environment. That excited my father very much.

As always, he used his magazine articles to create a dialog with his readers about his regenerative vision. The garden and farms he discussed in his articles became symbols not only for his readers' connection to their own gardens and farms but also for their connection to themselves and others. In this connection—between people working together to improve themselves and their world—my father saw solutions to the world's growing problems of famine and environmental degradation.

Knowing these solutions could be found in our connection to nature, he continued to travel throughout the world, learning what other people were doing and then sharing those success stories with as many people as he could. Again his competitive spirit kicked in: he knew he had much to do and little time to do it. He often wondered, "Am I doing enough?"

Not long before his death, I had the opportunity to travel with him to China. He had been there seventeen years earlier, and when we returned together, he was amazed at how much had changed. Beautiful images remembered from his first visit were ruined by the destruction of overpopulation and rampant development. I saw his enthusiasm for his dreams of a regenerative world begin to fade.

But my father was also a positive thinker. He was already thinking about his next article for *Organic Gardening* and how he could use our China visit and experience in a positive way for global improvement. Unfortunately, he never got a chance to see his China articles published. He was killed in an auto crash in Moscow on his way to the Moscow Airport after signing an agreement that would help start a magazine for farmers and gardeners in Russia. To the end, he never lost sight of his ability to communicate an important message to people around the world through the written word.

Three months before his trip to Moscow, my father wrote his last article for *Prevention*. At that point, he was definitely in the fourth phase of his life—his spiritual connection to the world around him. The article was entitled "Be Alive!" He started the article with a question about his father, J.I.: "Can a person be so alive that their friends expect to meet and talk with them years after their death? Possibly so! At least that happened to my father."

He went on to talk about his own life, saying, "One of the main ways to actually be more alive is to walk fearlessly just about anywhere." In his last few years, my father did exactly that. He walked the dangerous streets of Dakar, Senegal; he did the same in Ethiopia and many other countries, such as China, India, and Russia. "Nothing bad ever happened to me," he said in *Prevention*. "Far from it!"

That's a message we can all benefit from. In fact, it's the message of The Rodale Institute today. The Institute is the living voice of my father, grandfather, and future generations. We will continue to walk fearlessly, but in a determined way, building and growing on practical experience and the vision and spirit of the J.I. and Robert Rodale team.

WINTER

G A R D E N

M O N T H L Y

January

February

March

GARDENING

WINTER

MONDAY	TUESDAY	WEDNESDAY

TEMPERATURE	TEMPERATURE	TEMPERATURE
MAX./MIN. _____ °F/°C	MAX./MIN. _____ °F/°C	MAX./MIN. _____ °F/°C
PRECIPITATION	PRECIPITATION	PRECIPITATION
CONDITIONS	CONDITIONS	CONDITIONS
WIND	WIND	WIND
N NE E SE S SW W NW	N NE E SE S SW W NW	N NE E SE S SW W NW

Week of _____ *to* _____
(month, day)   (month, day)

THURSDAY	FRIDAY	SATURDAY	SUNDAY

TEMPERATURE | TEMPERATURE | TEMPERATURE | TEMPERATURE

MAX./MIN. _____ °F/°C | MAX./MIN. _____ °F/°C | MAX./MIN. _____ °F/°C | MAX./MIN. _____ °F/°C

PRECIPITATION | PRECIPITATION | PRECIPITATION | PRECIPITATION

CONDITIONS | CONDITIONS | CONDITIONS | CONDITIONS

WIND | WIND | WIND | WIND

N NE E SE S SW W NW | N NE E SE S SW W NW | N NE E SE S SW W NW | N NE E SE S SW W NW

WINTER

MONDAY	TUESDAY	WEDNESDAY	THURSDAY

TEMPERATURE

MAX./MIN. _____ °F/°C

PRECIPITATION

CONDITIONS

WIND

N NE E SE S SW W NW

TEMPERATURE

MAX./MIN. _____ °F/°C

PRECIPITATION

CONDITIONS

WIND

N NE E SE S SW W NW

TEMPERATURE

MAX./MIN. _____ °F/°C

PRECIPITATION

CONDITIONS

WIND

N NE E SE S SW W NW

TEMPERATURE

MAX./MIN. _____ °F/°C

PRECIPITATION

CONDITIONS

WIND

N NE E SE S SW W NW

Week of _____ *to* _____
(month, day)   (month, day)

FRIDAY	SATURDAY	SUNDAY

TEMPERATURE

MAX./MIN. _____ °F/°C

PRECIPITATION

CONDITIONS

WIND

N NE E SE S SW W NW

TEMPERATURE

MAX./MIN. _____ °F/°C

PRECIPITATION

CONDITIONS

WIND

N NE E SE S SW W NW

TEMPERATURE

MAX./MIN. _____ °F/°C

PRECIPITATION

CONDITIONS

WIND

N NE E SE S SW W NW

"Unseen buds, infinite, hidden well, Under the snow and ice, under the darkness, in every square or cubic inch, Germinal, exquisite, in delicate lace, microscopic unborn, like babes in wombs, latent, folded, compact, sleeping . . ."
WALT WHITMAN

WINTER

MONDAY	TUESDAY	WEDNESDAY

Be prepared for the coming year's harvest by reading up on preserving, drying, and curing techniques.

TEMPERATURE	TEMPERATURE	TEMPERATURE
MAX./MIN. _____ °F/°C	MAX./MIN. _____ °F/°C	MAX./MIN. _____ °F/°C
PRECIPITATION	PRECIPITATION	PRECIPITATION
CONDITIONS	CONDITIONS	CONDITIONS
WIND	WIND	WIND
N NE E SE S SW W NW	N NE E SE S SW W NW	N NE E SE S SW W NW

Week of _____ *to* _____
      (month, day)   (month, day)

THURSDAY	FRIDAY	SATURDAY	SUNDAY

TEMPERATURE	TEMPERATURE	TEMPERATURE	TEMPERATURE
MAX./MIN. _____ °F/°C	MAX./MIN. _____ °F/°C	MAX./MIN. _____ °F/°C	MAX./MIN. _____ °F/°C
PRECIPITATION	PRECIPITATION	PRECIPITATION	PRECIPITATION
CONDITIONS	CONDITIONS	CONDITIONS	CONDITIONS
WIND	WIND	WIND	WIND
N NE E SE S SW W NW	N NE E SE S SW W NW	N NE E SE S SW W NW	N NE E SE S SW W NW

WINTER

MONDAY	TUESDAY	WEDNESDAY	THURSDAY

TEMPERATURE

MAX./MIN. _____ °F/°C

PRECIPITATION

CONDITIONS

WIND

N NE E SE S SW W NW

TEMPERATURE

MAX./MIN. _____ °F/°C

PRECIPITATION

CONDITIONS

WIND

N NE E SE S SW W NW

TEMPERATURE

MAX./MIN. _____ °F/°C

PRECIPITATION

CONDITIONS

WIND

N NE E SE S SW W NW

TEMPERATURE

MAX./MIN. _____ °F/°C

PRECIPITATION

CONDITIONS

WIND

N NE E SE S SW W NW

Week of _____ *to* _____
(month, day)   (month, day)

FRIDAY	SATURDAY	SUNDAY

"In a way winter is the
real spring, the time when
the inner thing happens.
The resurge of nature."
EDNA O'BRIEN

TEMPERATURE	TEMPERATURE	TEMPERATURE
MAX./MIN. _____ °F/°C	MAX./MIN. _____ °F/°C	MAX./MIN. _____ °F/°C
PRECIPITATION	PRECIPITATION	PRECIPITATION
CONDITIONS	CONDITIONS	CONDITIONS
WIND	WIND	WIND
N NE E SE S SW W NW	N NE E SE S SW W NW	N NE E SE S SW W NW

WINTER

MONDAY	TUESDAY	WEDNESDAY

Find out about your backyard's microclimates. The more you know, the more you'll grow. Consider past weather trends as well as the future's. For more information contact your local agriculture extension office.

TEMPERATURE	TEMPERATURE	TEMPERATURE
MAX./MIN. _____ °F/°C	MAX./MIN. _____ °F/°C	MAX./MIN. _____ °F/°C
PRECIPITATION	PRECIPITATION	PRECIPITATION
CONDITIONS	CONDITIONS	CONDITIONS
WIND	WIND	WIND
N NE E SE S SW W NW	N NE E SE S SW W NW	N NE E SE S SW W NW

Week of _____ *to* _____
(month, day)   *(month, day)*

THURSDAY	FRIDAY	SATURDAY	SUNDAY

TEMPERATURE	TEMPERATURE	TEMPERATURE	TEMPERATURE
MAX./MIN. _____ °F/°C	MAX./MIN. _____ °F/°C	MAX./MIN. _____ °F/°C	MAX./MIN. _____ °F/°C

PRECIPITATION   **PRECIPITATION**   **PRECIPITATION**   **PRECIPITATION**

CONDITIONS   **CONDITIONS**   **CONDITIONS**   **CONDITIONS**

WIND   **WIND**   **WIND**   **WIND**

N NE E SE S SW W NW   N NE E SE S SW W NW   N NE E SE S SW W NW   N NE E SE S SW W NW

W I N T E R

MONDAY	TUESDAY	WEDNESDAY	THURSDAY

TEMPERATURE

MAX./MIN. _____ °F/°C

PRECIPITATION

CONDITIONS

WIND

N NE E SE S SW W NW

TEMPERATURE

MAX./MIN. _____ °F/°C

PRECIPITATION

CONDITIONS

WIND

N NE E SE S SW W NW

TEMPERATURE

MAX./MIN. _____ °F/°C

PRECIPITATION

CONDITIONS

WIND

N NE E SE S SW W NW

TEMPERATURE

MAX./MIN. _____ °F/°C

PRECIPITATION

CONDITIONS

WIND

N NE E SE S SW W NW

FRIDAY	SATURDAY	SUNDAY

> *"Blackberry winter, the time when the hoarfrost lies on the blackberry blossoms; without this frost the berries will not set. It is the forerunner of a rich harvest."*
>
> MARGARET MEAD

TEMPERATURE	TEMPERATURE	TEMPERATURE
MAX./MIN. _____ °F/°C	MAX./MIN. _____ °F/°C	MAX./MIN. _____ °F/°C
PRECIPITATION	PRECIPITATION	PRECIPITATION
CONDITIONS	CONDITIONS	CONDITIONS
WIND	WIND	WIND
N NE E SE S SW W NW	N NE E SE S SW W NW	N NE E SE S SW W NW

WINTER

MONDAY	TUESDAY	WEDNESDAY

A barren winter yard provides a great blueprint for the design of a garden. Fill in the lifeless void with a harvest of color in your mind. Consider the sun's exposure to your property throughout the day, as well as if there is adequate rain drainage when it's not shining.

MONDAY

TEMPERATURE

MAX./MIN. _____ °F/°C

PRECIPITATION

CONDITIONS

WIND

N NE E SE S SW W NW

TUESDAY

TEMPERATURE

MAX./MIN. _____ °F/°C

PRECIPITATION

CONDITIONS

WIND

N NE E SE S SW W NW

WEDNESDAY

TEMPERATURE

MAX./MIN. _____ °F/°C

PRECIPITATION

CONDITIONS

WIND

N NE E SE S SW W NW

Week of _____ *to* _____
(month, day)   (month, day)

THURSDAY	FRIDAY	SATURDAY	SUNDAY

TEMPERATURE | TEMPERATURE | TEMPERATURE | TEMPERATURE

MAX./MIN. _____ °F/°C   MAX./MIN. _____ °F/°C   MAX./MIN. _____ °F/°C   MAX./MIN. _____ °F/°C

PRECIPITATION | PRECIPITATION | PRECIPITATION | PRECIPITATION

CONDITIONS | CONDITIONS | CONDITIONS | CONDITIONS

WIND | WIND | WIND | WIND

N NE E SE S SW W NW   N NE E SE S SW W NW   N NE E SE S SW W NW   N NE E SE S SW W NW

WINTER

MONDAY	TUESDAY	WEDNESDAY	THURSDAY

TEMPERATURE

MAX./MIN. _____ °F/°C

PRECIPITATION

CONDITIONS

WIND

N NE E SE S SW W NW

TEMPERATURE

MAX./MIN. _____ °F/°C

PRECIPITATION

CONDITIONS

WIND

N NE E SE S SW W NW

TEMPERATURE

MAX./MIN. _____ °F/°C

PRECIPITATION

CONDITIONS

WIND

N NE E SE S SW W NW

TEMPERATURE

MAX./MIN. _____ °F/°C

PRECIPITATION

CONDITIONS

WIND

N NE E SE S SW W NW

Week of _____ *to* _____
(month, day)   (month, day)

FRIDAY	SATURDAY	SUNDAY

"*The farmer in
deep thought
is pacing through the rain
among his blank fields,
with
hands in pockets,
in his head
the harvest already
planted.*"
WILLIAM CARLOS WILLIAMS

TEMPERATURE	TEMPERATURE	TEMPERATURE
MAX./MIN. _____ °F/°C	MAX./MIN. _____ °F/°C	MAX./MIN. _____ °F/°C
PRECIPITATION	PRECIPITATION	PRECIPITATION
CONDITIONS	CONDITIONS	CONDITIONS
WIND	WIND	WIND
N NE E SE S SW W NW	N NE E SE S SW W NW	N NE E SE S SW W NW

WINTER

MONDAY	TUESDAY	WEDNESDAY

Everyone could use a hand in maintaining a garden. Employ birds to prey upon harmful bugs by attracting them with bird feeders and a water supply in winter. Come summer they will repay your kindness tenfold.

TEMPERATURE	TEMPERATURE	TEMPERATURE
MAX./MIN. _____ °F/°C	MAX./MIN. _____ °F/°C	MAX./MIN. _____ °F/°C
PRECIPITATION	PRECIPITATION	PRECIPITATION
CONDITIONS	CONDITIONS	CONDITIONS
WIND	WIND	WIND
N NE E SE S SW W NW	N NE E SE S SW W NW	N NE E SE S SW W NW

Week of _____ *to* _____
(month, day)   *(month, day)*

THURSDAY	FRIDAY	SATURDAY	SUNDAY

TEMPERATURE	TEMPERATURE	TEMPERATURE	TEMPERATURE
MAX./MIN. _____ °F/°C	MAX./MIN. _____ °F/°C	MAX./MIN. _____ °F/°C	MAX./MIN. _____ °F/°C

PRECIPITATION

CONDITIONS

WIND

N NE E SE S SW W NW   N NE E SE S SW W NW   N NE E SE S SW W NW   N NE E SE S SW W NW

WINTER

MONDAY	TUESDAY	WEDNESDAY	THURSDAY

TEMPERATURE

MAX./MIN. _____ °F/°C

PRECIPITATION

CONDITIONS

WIND

N NE E SE S SW W NW

TEMPERATURE

MAX./MIN. _____ °F/°C

PRECIPITATION

CONDITIONS

WIND

N NE E SE S SW W NW

TEMPERATURE

MAX./MIN. _____ °F/°C

PRECIPITATION

CONDITIONS

WIND

N NE E SE S SW W NW

TEMPERATURE

MAX./MIN. _____ °F/°C

PRECIPITATION

CONDITIONS

WIND

N NE E SE S SW W NW

FRIDAY	SATURDAY	SUNDAY

"All they could see was sky,
water, birds, light and
confluence.
It was the whole morning
world."
EUDORA WELTY

TEMPERATURE	TEMPERATURE	TEMPERATURE
MAX./MIN. _____ °F/°C	MAX./MIN. _____ °F/°C	MAX./MIN. _____ °F/°C
PRECIPITATION	PRECIPITATION	PRECIPITATION
CONDITIONS	CONDITIONS	CONDITIONS
WIND	WIND	WIND
N NE E SE S SW W NW	N NE E SE S SW W NW	N NE E SE S SW W NW

WINTER

MONDAY	TUESDAY	WEDNESDAY

As winter retreats, weeds advance. Dig them up now before they become established fixtures in your spring garden.

Get seeds and plant labels together, and start indoors on tomatoes, onions, cabbages, and peppers. Give them prime window space to soak up the sun.

TEMPERATURE	TEMPERATURE	TEMPERATURE
MAX./MIN. _____ °F/°C	MAX./MIN. _____ °F/°C	MAX./MIN. _____ °F/°C
PRECIPITATION	PRECIPITATION	PRECIPITATION
CONDITIONS	CONDITIONS	CONDITIONS
WIND	WIND	WIND
N NE E SE S SW W NW	N NE E SE S SW W NW	N NE E SE S SW W NW

Week of _____ *to* _____
(month, day)   (month, day)

THURSDAY	FRIDAY	SATURDAY	SUNDAY

TEMPERATURE

MAX./MIN. _____ °F/°C

PRECIPITATION

CONDITIONS

WIND

N NE E SE S SW W NW

TEMPERATURE

MAX./MIN. _____ °F/°C

PRECIPITATION

CONDITIONS

WIND

N NE E SE S SW W NW

TEMPERATURE

MAX./MIN. _____ °F/°C

PRECIPITATION

CONDITIONS

WIND

N NE E SE S SW W NW

TEMPERATURE

MAX./MIN. _____ °F/°C

PRECIPITATION

CONDITIONS

WIND

N NE E SE S SW W NW

WINTER

MONDAY	TUESDAY	WEDNESDAY	THURSDAY

TEMPERATURE

MAX./MIN. _____ °F/°C

PRECIPITATION

CONDITIONS

WIND

N NE E SE S SW W NW

TEMPERATURE

MAX./MIN. _____ °F/°C

PRECIPITATION

CONDITIONS

WIND

N NE E SE S SW W NW

TEMPERATURE

MAX./MIN. _____ °F/°C

PRECIPITATION

CONDITIONS

WIND

N NE E SE S SW W NW

TEMPERATURE

MAX./MIN. _____ °F/°C

PRECIPITATION

CONDITIONS

WIND

N NE E SE S SW W NW

Week of _____ *to* _____
(month, day)   (month, day)

FRIDAY	SATURDAY	SUNDAY

"During March while
hoeing long rows of cotton
Dirt lifted in the air
Entering my nostrils
And eyes
The yellow under my
fingernails"
GARY SOTO

TEMPERATURE

MAX./MIN. _____ °F/°C

PRECIPITATION

CONDITIONS

WIND

N NE E SE S SW W NW

TEMPERATURE

MAX./MIN. _____ °F/°C

PRECIPITATION

CONDITIONS

WIND

N NE E SE S SW W NW

TEMPERATURE

MAX./MIN. _____ °F/°C

PRECIPITATION

CONDITIONS

WIND

N NE E SE S SW W NW

S P R I N G

PLANNING

GARDEN
PLANNING

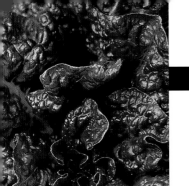

MONTHLY

April

May

June

GARDENING

SPRING

MONDAY	TUESDAY	WEDNESDAY

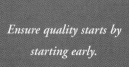

Ensure quality starts by starting early.

Start digging your garden, adding cured fall compost and organic fertilizer.

TEMPERATURE	TEMPERATURE	TEMPERATURE
MAX./MIN. _____ °F/°C	MAX./MIN. _____ °F/°C	MAX./MIN. _____ °F/°C
PRECIPITATION	PRECIPITATION	PRECIPITATION
CONDITIONS	CONDITIONS	CONDITIONS
WIND	WIND	WIND
N NE E SE S SW W NW	N NE E SE S SW W NW	N NE E SE S SW W NW

Week of _____ *to* _____
(month, day)   (month, day)

THURSDAY	FRIDAY	SATURDAY	SUNDAY

TEMPERATURE

MAX./MIN. _____ °F/°C

PRECIPITATION

CONDITIONS

WIND

N NE E SE S SW W NW

TEMPERATURE

MAX./MIN. _____ °F/°C

PRECIPITATION

CONDITIONS

WIND

N NE E SE S SW W NW

TEMPERATURE

MAX./MIN. _____ °F/°C

PRECIPITATION

CONDITIONS

WIND

N NE E SE S SW W NW

TEMPERATURE

MAX./MIN. _____ °F/°C

PRECIPITATION

CONDITIONS

WIND

N NE E SE S SW W NW

SPRING

MONDAY	TUESDAY	WEDNESDAY	THURSDAY

TEMPERATURE

MAX./MIN. _____ °F/°C

PRECIPITATION

CONDITIONS

WIND

N NE E SE S SW W NW

TEMPERATURE

MAX./MIN. _____ °F/°C

PRECIPITATION

CONDITIONS

WIND

N NE E SE S SW W NW

TEMPERATURE

MAX./MIN. _____ °F/°C

PRECIPITATION

CONDITIONS

WIND

N NE E SE S SW W NW

TEMPERATURE

MAX./MIN. _____ °F/°C

PRECIPITATION

CONDITIONS

WIND

N NE E SE S SW W NW

FRIDAY	SATURDAY	SUNDAY

"Spring came on forever,
Spring came on forever,
Said the Chinese
nightingale."
VACHEL LINDSAY

TEMPERATURE	TEMPERATURE	TEMPERATURE
MAX./MIN. _____ °F/°C	MAX./MIN. _____ °F/°C	MAX./MIN. _____ °F/°C
PRECIPITATION	PRECIPITATION	PRECIPITATION
CONDITIONS	CONDITIONS	CONDITIONS
WIND	WIND	WIND
N NE E SE S SW W NW	N NE E SE S SW W NW	N NE E SE S SW W NW

SPRING

MONDAY	TUESDAY	WEDNESDAY

Mulch plants to smother weeds and to help the soil retain water.

Get your planting beds in order. Consider benefits of crop placement other than appearance. For example, grow marigolds by tomatoes to reduce the risk of aphids.

TEMPERATURE	TEMPERATURE	TEMPERATURE
MAX./MIN. _____ °F/°C	MAX./MIN. _____ °F/°C	MAX./MIN. _____ °F/°C
PRECIPITATION	PRECIPITATION	PRECIPITATION
CONDITIONS	CONDITIONS	CONDITIONS
WIND	WIND	WIND
N NE E SE S SW W NW	N NE E SE S SW W NW	N NE E SE S SW W NW

Week of _____ *to* _____

THURSDAY	FRIDAY	SATURDAY	SUNDAY
TEMPERATURE	TEMPERATURE	TEMPERATURE	TEMPERATURE
MAX./MIN. _____ °F/°C	MAX./MIN. _____ °F/°C	MAX./MIN. _____ °F/°C	MAX./MIN. _____ °F/°C
PRECIPITATION	PRECIPITATION	PRECIPITATION	PRECIPITATION
CONDITIONS	CONDITIONS	CONDITIONS	CONDITIONS
WIND	WIND	WIND	WIND
N NE E SE S SW W NW	N NE E SE S SW W NW	N NE E SE S SW W NW	N NE E SE S SW W NW

S P R I N G

MONDAY	TUESDAY	WEDNESDAY	THURSDAY

TEMPERATURE

MAX./MIN. _____ °F/°C

PRECIPITATION

CONDITIONS

WIND

N NE E SE S SW W NW

TEMPERATURE

MAX./MIN. _____ °F/°C

PRECIPITATION

CONDITIONS

WIND

N NE E SE S SW W NW

TEMPERATURE

MAX./MIN. _____ °F/°C

PRECIPITATION

CONDITIONS

WIND

N NE E SE S SW W NW

TEMPERATURE

MAX./MIN. _____ °F/°C

PRECIPITATION

CONDITIONS

WIND

N NE E SE S SW W NW

Week of _____ to _____
(month, day)   (month, day)

FRIDAY	SATURDAY	SUNDAY

*"And the new plants, still
awkward in their soil,
The lovely diminutives.
I could watch!
I could watch!
I saw the separateness of
all things!"*
THEODORE ROETHKE

FRIDAY

TEMPERATURE

MAX./MIN. _____ °F/°C

PRECIPITATION

CONDITIONS

WIND

N NE E SE S SW W NW

SATURDAY

TEMPERATURE

MAX./MIN. _____ °F/°C

PRECIPITATION

CONDITIONS

WIND

N NE E SE S SW W NW

SUNDAY

TEMPERATURE

MAX./MIN. _____ °F/°C

PRECIPITATION

CONDITIONS

WIND

N NE E SE S SW W NW

S P R I N G

MONDAY	TUESDAY	WEDNESDAY

When transplanting starts, prepare them for the rough adjustment to the outdoors by breaking them in gradually. Set them outside a few hours at a time to ease the transition.

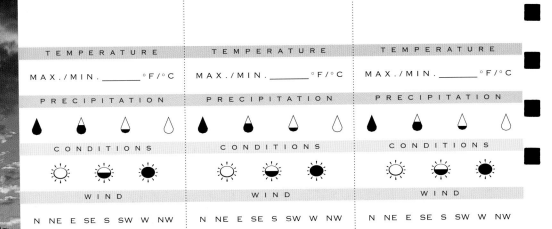

TEMPERATURE	TEMPERATURE	TEMPERATURE
MAX./MIN. _____ °F/°C	MAX./MIN. _____ °F/°C	MAX./MIN. _____ °F/°C
PRECIPITATION	PRECIPITATION	PRECIPITATION
CONDITIONS	CONDITIONS	CONDITIONS
WIND	WIND	WIND
N NE E SE S SW W NW	N NE E SE S SW W NW	N NE E SE S SW W NW

THURSDAY	FRIDAY	SATURDAY	SUNDAY

TEMPERATURE | TEMPERATURE | TEMPERATURE | TEMPERATURE

MAX./MIN. _____°F/°C | MAX./MIN. _____°F/°C | MAX./MIN. _____°F/°C | MAX./MIN. _____°F/°C

PRECIPITATION | PRECIPITATION | PRECIPITATION | PRECIPITATION

CONDITIONS | CONDITIONS | CONDITIONS | CONDITIONS

WIND | WIND | WIND | WIND

N NE E SE S SW W NW | N NE E SE S SW W NW | N NE E SE S SW W NW | N NE E SE S SW W NW

S P R I N G

MONDAY	TUESDAY	WEDNESDAY	THURSDAY

TEMPERATURE	TEMPERATURE	TEMPERATURE	TEMPERATURE
MAX./MIN. _____ °F/°C	MAX./MIN. _____ °F/°C	MAX./MIN. _____ °F/°C	MAX./MIN. _____ °F/°C
PRECIPITATION	PRECIPITATION	PRECIPITATION	PRECIPITATION
CONDITIONS	CONDITIONS	CONDITIONS	CONDITIONS
WIND	WIND	WIND	WIND
N NE E SE S SW W NW	N NE E SE S SW W NW	N NE E SE S SW W NW	N NE E SE S SW W NW

Week of _____ to _____
(month, day)   (month, day)

FRIDAY	SATURDAY	SUNDAY

TEMPERATURE

MAX./MIN. _____ °F/°C

PRECIPITATION

CONDITIONS

WIND

N NE E SE S SW W NW

TEMPERATURE

MAX./MIN. _____ °F/°C

PRECIPITATION

CONDITIONS

WIND

N NE E SE S SW W NW

TEMPERATURE

MAX./MIN. _____ °F/°C

PRECIPITATION

CONDITIONS

WIND

N NE E SE S SW W NW

"Up against the wind that
measures spring
and entering cold with a
fist around the hoe
and leveling what was a
hill into an irrigated flow."
LARRY GOODELL

S P R I N G

MONDAY	TUESDAY	WEDNESDAY

Give seeds their best chance by planting them at a depth of two to three times their width. Cover them, and keep them moist.

Keep an eye to the sky, particularly the week before a full moon, which can bring late frosts.

TEMPERATURE

MAX./MIN. _____ °F/°C

PRECIPITATION

CONDITIONS

WIND

N NE E SE S SW W NW

TEMPERATURE

MAX./MIN. _____ °F/°C

PRECIPITATION

CONDITIONS

WIND

N NE E SE S SW W NW

TEMPERATURE

MAX./MIN. _____ °F/°C

PRECIPITATION

CONDITIONS

WIND

N NE E SE S SW W NW

THURSDAY	FRIDAY	SATURDAY	SUNDAY
TEMPERATURE	TEMPERATURE	TEMPERATURE	TEMPERATURE
MAX./MIN. _____ °F/°C	MAX./MIN. _____ °F/°C	MAX./MIN. _____ °F/°C	MAX./MIN. _____ °F/°C
PRECIPITATION	PRECIPITATION	PRECIPITATION	PRECIPITATION
CONDITIONS	CONDITIONS	CONDITIONS	CONDITIONS
WIND	WIND	WIND	WIND
N NE E SE S SW W NW	N NE E SE S SW W NW	N NE E SE S SW W NW	N NE E SE S SW W NW

SPRING

MONDAY	TUESDAY	WEDNESDAY	THURSDAY

TEMPERATURE

MAX./MIN. _____ °F/°C

PRECIPITATION

CONDITIONS

WIND

N NE E SE S SW W NW

TEMPERATURE

MAX./MIN. _____ °F/°C

PRECIPITATION

CONDITIONS

WIND

N NE E SE S SW W NW

TEMPERATURE

MAX./MIN. _____ °F/°C

PRECIPITATION

CONDITIONS

WIND

N NE E SE S SW W NW

TEMPERATURE

MAX./MIN. _____ °F/°C

PRECIPITATION

CONDITIONS

WIND

N NE E SE S SW W NW

FRIDAY	SATURDAY	SUNDAY

"The May sun—Whom
All things imitate—
that glues small leaves to
the wooden trees"
WILLIAM CARLOS WILLIAMS

TEMPERATURE	TEMPERATURE	TEMPERATURE
MAX./MIN. _____ °F/°C	MAX./MIN. _____ °F/°C	MAX./MIN. _____ °F/°C
PRECIPITATION	PRECIPITATION	PRECIPITATION
CONDITIONS	CONDITIONS	CONDITIONS
WIND	WIND	WIND
N NE E SE S SW W NW	N NE E SE S SW W NW	N NE E SE S SW W NW

SPRING

MONDAY	TUESDAY	WEDNESDAY

All bugs aren't bad for the garden. Attract beneficial bugs to set up a system of natural pest control that is free of harmful insecticides.

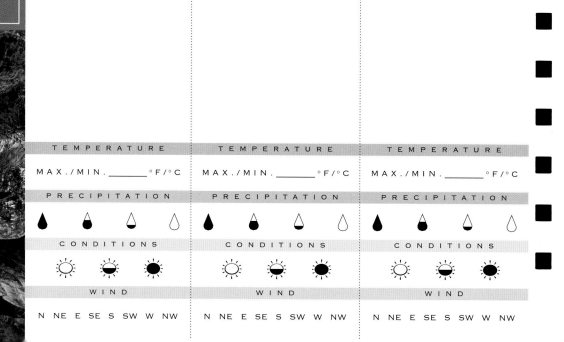

TEMPERATURE	TEMPERATURE	TEMPERATURE
MAX./MIN. _____ °F/°C	MAX./MIN. _____ °F/°C	MAX./MIN. _____ °F/°C
PRECIPITATION	PRECIPITATION	PRECIPITATION
CONDITIONS	CONDITIONS	CONDITIONS
WIND	WIND	WIND
N NE E SE S SW W NW	N NE E SE S SW W NW	N NE E SE S SW W NW

Week of _____ *to* _____
(month, day)   (month, day)

THURSDAY	FRIDAY	SATURDAY	SUNDAY

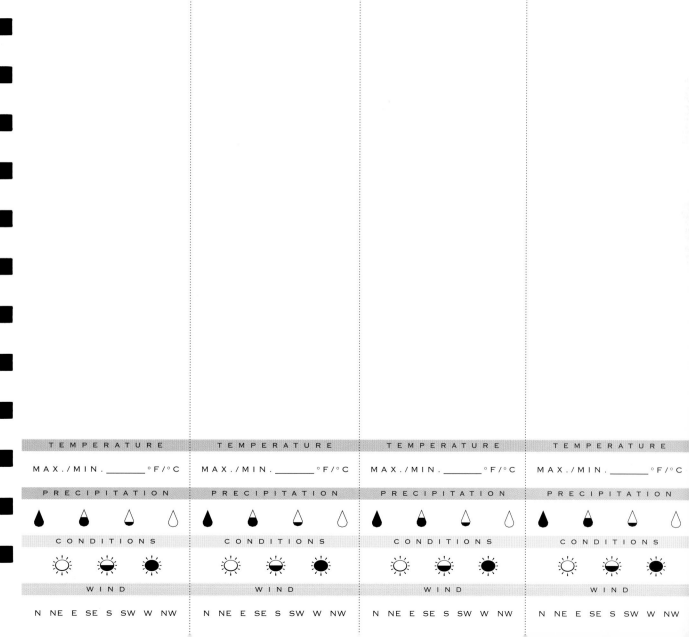

TEMPERATURE

MAX./MIN. _____ °F/°C

PRECIPITATION

CONDITIONS

WIND

N NE E SE S SW W NW

TEMPERATURE

MAX./MIN. _____ °F/°C

PRECIPITATION

CONDITIONS

WIND

N NE E SE S SW W NW

TEMPERATURE

MAX./MIN. _____ °F/°C

PRECIPITATION

CONDITIONS

WIND

N NE E SE S SW W NW

TEMPERATURE

MAX./MIN. _____ °F/°C

PRECIPITATION

CONDITIONS

WIND

N NE E SE S SW W NW

SPRING

MONDAY	TUESDAY	WEDNESDAY	THURSDAY

TEMPERATURE

MAX./MIN. _____ °F/°C

PRECIPITATION

CONDITIONS

WIND

N NE E SE S SW W NW

TEMPERATURE

MAX./MIN. _____ °F/°C

PRECIPITATION

CONDITIONS

WIND

N NE E SE S SW W NW

TEMPERATURE

MAX./MIN. _____ °F/°C

PRECIPITATION

CONDITIONS

WIND

N NE E SE S SW W NW

TEMPERATURE

MAX./MIN. _____ °F/°C

PRECIPITATION

CONDITIONS

WIND

N NE E SE S SW W NW

Week of _____ *to* _____

FRIDAY	SATURDAY	SUNDAY

"O our Mother the Earth,
Our Father the Sky,
Your children are we, and
with tired backs
We bring you gifts."
SONG OF THE SKY LOOM
(TEWA)

TEMPERATURE	TEMPERATURE	TEMPERATURE
MAX./MIN. _____ °F/°C	MAX./MIN. _____ °F/°C	MAX./MIN. _____ °F/°C
PRECIPITATION	PRECIPITATION	PRECIPITATION
CONDITIONS	CONDITIONS	CONDITIONS
WIND	WIND	WIND
N NE E SE S SW W NW	N NE E SE S SW W NW	N NE E SE S SW W NW

S P R I N G

MONDAY　　　　**TUESDAY**　　　　**WEDNESDAY**

Make sure to add continually to your compost pile. You'll need three equal parts of brown vegetation, green vegetation, and soil. All of these ingredients are for the most part free and can be found in your kitchen trash or in the confines of your yard.

TEMPERATURE	TEMPERATURE	TEMPERATURE
MAX./MIN. _____ °F/°C	MAX./MIN. _____ °F/°C	MAX./MIN. _____ °F/°C

PRECIPITATION	PRECIPITATION	PRECIPITATION

CONDITIONS	CONDITIONS	CONDITIONS

WIND	WIND	WIND
N NE E SE S SW W NW	N NE E SE S SW W NW	N NE E SE S SW W NW

Week of _____ *to* _____
(month, day)   (month, day)

THURSDAY	FRIDAY	SATURDAY	SUNDAY

TEMPERATURE

MAX./MIN. _____ °F/°C   MAX./MIN. _____ °F/°C   MAX./MIN. _____ °F/°C   MAX./MIN. _____ °F/°C

PRECIPITATION

CONDITIONS

WIND

N NE E SE S SW W NW   N NE E SE S SW W NW   N NE E SE S SW W NW   N NE E SE S SW W NW

SPRING

MONDAY	TUESDAY	WEDNESDAY	THURSDAY

TEMPERATURE	TEMPERATURE	TEMPERATURE	TEMPERATURE
MAX./MIN. _____ °F/°C	MAX./MIN. _____ °F/°C	MAX./MIN. _____ °F/°C	MAX./MIN. _____ °F/°C
PRECIPITATION	PRECIPITATION	PRECIPITATION	PRECIPITATION
CONDITIONS	CONDITIONS	CONDITIONS	CONDITIONS
WIND	WIND	WIND	WIND
N NE E SE S SW W NW	N NE E SE S SW W NW	N NE E SE S SW W NW	N NE E SE S SW W NW

FRIDAY	SATURDAY	SUNDAY

"Draw over and dig
The loose ash soil
Hoe handles are short,
The sun's course long
Fingers deep in the
earth search
Roots, pull them out,
feel through;
Roots are strong."

GARY SNYDER

TEMPERATURE	TEMPERATURE	TEMPERATURE
MAX./MIN. _____ °F/°C	MAX./MIN. _____ °F/°C	MAX./MIN. _____ °F/°C
PRECIPITATION	PRECIPITATION	PRECIPITATION
CONDITIONS	CONDITIONS	CONDITIONS
WIND	WIND	WIND
N NE E SE S SW W NW	N NE E SE S SW W NW	N NE E SE S SW W NW

SPRING

MONDAY	TUESDAY	WEDNESDAY

Make weeding a priority. Switch from a standard hoe to a hula hoe and see what you have been missing. Learn to master this tool and your crops will benefit.

TEMPERATURE	TEMPERATURE	TEMPERATURE
MAX./MIN. _____ °F/°C	MAX./MIN. _____ °F/°C	MAX./MIN. _____ °F/°C
PRECIPITATION	PRECIPITATION	PRECIPITATION
CONDITIONS	CONDITIONS	CONDITIONS
WIND	WIND	WIND
N NE E SE S SW W NW	N NE E SE S SW W NW	N NE E SE S SW W NW

Week of _____ *to* _____
(month, day)   (month, day)

THURSDAY	FRIDAY	SATURDAY	SUNDAY

TEMPERATURE

MAX./MIN. _____ °F/°C

PRECIPITATION

CONDITIONS

WIND

N NE E SE S SW W NW

TEMPERATURE

MAX./MIN. _____ °F/°C

PRECIPITATION

CONDITIONS

WIND

N NE E SE S SW W NW

TEMPERATURE

MAX./MIN. _____ °F/°C

PRECIPITATION

CONDITIONS

WIND

N NE E SE S SW W NW

TEMPERATURE

MAX./MIN. _____ °F/°C

PRECIPITATION

CONDITIONS

WIND

N NE E SE S SW W NW

SUMMER

G A R D E N
PLANNING

MONTHLY

July

August

September

GARDENING

SUMMER

MONDAY	TUESDAY	WEDNESDAY

Keep the birds feeding on harmful insects and not your plants by installing netting over the crops you want protected. A cage-like construction works best.

TEMPERATURE	TEMPERATURE	TEMPERATURE
MAX./MIN. _____ °F/°C	MAX./MIN. _____ °F/°C	MAX./MIN. _____ °F/°C
PRECIPITATION	PRECIPITATION	PRECIPITATION
CONDITIONS	CONDITIONS	CONDITIONS
WIND	WIND	WIND
N NE E SE S SW W NW	N NE E SE S SW W NW	N NE E SE S SW W NW

THURSDAY	FRIDAY	SATURDAY	SUNDAY

TEMPERATURE	TEMPERATURE	TEMPERATURE	TEMPERATURE
MAX./MIN. _____ °F/°C	MAX./MIN. _____ °F/°C	MAX./MIN. _____ °F/°C	MAX./MIN. _____ °F/°C

PRECIPITATION · PRECIPITATION · PRECIPITATION · PRECIPITATION

CONDITIONS · CONDITIONS · CONDITIONS · CONDITIONS

WIND · WIND · WIND · WIND

N NE E SE S SW W NW   N NE E SE S SW W NW   N NE E SE S SW W NW   N NE E SE S SW W NW

SUMMER

MONDAY	TUESDAY	WEDNESDAY	THURSDAY

TEMPERATURE

MAX./MIN. _____ °F/°C

PRECIPITATION

CONDITIONS

WIND

N NE E SE S SW W NW

TEMPERATURE

MAX./MIN. _____ °F/°C

PRECIPITATION

CONDITIONS

WIND

N NE E SE S SW W NW

TEMPERATURE

MAX./MIN. _____ °F/°C

PRECIPITATION

CONDITIONS

WIND

N NE E SE S SW W NW

TEMPERATURE

MAX./MIN. _____ °F/°C

PRECIPITATION

CONDITIONS

WIND

N NE E SE S SW W NW

Week of _____ *to* _____
(month, day)   (month, day)

FRIDAY	SATURDAY	SUNDAY

TEMPERATURE	TEMPERATURE	TEMPERATURE
MAX./MIN. _____ °F/°C	MAX./MIN. _____ °F/°C	MAX./MIN. _____ °F/°C
PRECIPITATION	PRECIPITATION	PRECIPITATION
CONDITIONS	CONDITIONS	CONDITIONS
WIND	WIND	WIND
N NE E SE S SW W NW	N NE E SE S SW W NW	N NE E SE S SW W NW

SUMMER

MONDAY	TUESDAY	WEDNESDAY

*Begin to eye your plants
with patient hunger.
Gather recipes for the time
when they will transform
from plants into
tantalizing cuisine.*

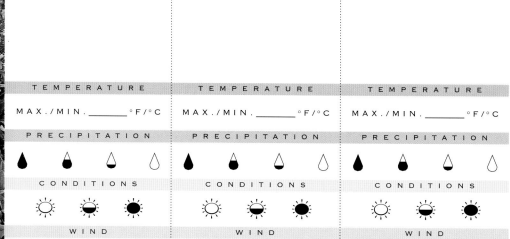

TEMPERATURE	TEMPERATURE	TEMPERATURE
MAX./MIN. _____ °F/°C	MAX./MIN. _____ °F/°C	MAX./MIN. _____ °F/°C
PRECIPITATION	PRECIPITATION	PRECIPITATION
CONDITIONS	CONDITIONS	CONDITIONS
WIND	WIND	WIND
N NE E SE S SW W NW	N NE E SE S SW W NW	N NE E SE S SW W NW

Week of _____ *to* _____
(month, day)   (month, day)

THURSDAY	FRIDAY	SATURDAY	SUNDAY

TEMPERATURE

MAX./MIN. _____ °F/°C

PRECIPITATION

CONDITIONS

WIND

N NE E SE S SW W NW

TEMPERATURE

MAX./MIN. _____ °F/°C

PRECIPITATION

CONDITIONS

WIND

N NE E SE S SW W NW

TEMPERATURE

MAX./MIN. _____ °F/°C

PRECIPITATION

CONDITIONS

WIND

N NE E SE S SW W NW

TEMPERATURE

MAX./MIN. _____ °F/°C

PRECIPITATION

CONDITIONS

WIND

N NE E SE S SW W NW

SUMMER

MONDAY	TUESDAY	WEDNESDAY	THURSDAY

TEMPERATURE

MAX./MIN. _____ °F / °C

PRECIPITATION

CONDITIONS

WIND

N NE E SE S SW W NW

TEMPERATURE

MAX./MIN. _____ °F / °C

PRECIPITATION

CONDITIONS

WIND

N NE E SE S SW W NW

TEMPERATURE

MAX./MIN. _____ °F / °C

PRECIPITATION

CONDITIONS

WIND

N NE E SE S SW W NW

TEMPERATURE

MAX./MIN. _____ °F / °C

PRECIPITATION

CONDITIONS

WIND

N NE E SE S SW W NW

FRIDAY	SATURDAY	SUNDAY

"Winds of Summer fields
Recollect the way—
Instinct picking up the key
Dropped by memory—"
EMILY DICKINSON

TEMPERATURE	TEMPERATURE	TEMPERATURE
MAX./MIN. _____ °F/°C	MAX./MIN. _____ °F/°C	MAX./MIN. _____ °F/°C
PRECIPITATION	PRECIPITATION	PRECIPITATION
CONDITIONS	CONDITIONS	CONDITIONS
WIND	WIND	WIND
N NE E SE S SW W NW	N NE E SE S SW W NW	N NE E SE S SW W NW

SUMMER

MONDAY	TUESDAY	WEDNESDAY

Resist using harmful chemicals for short-term gains. The top soil is like the tip of an iceberg and chemicals will kill not only unwanted plants and insects but also the millions of microorganisms below the surface—hard at work for you and your plants.

TEMPERATURE

MAX./MIN. _____ °F/°C

PRECIPITATION

CONDITIONS

WIND

N NE E SE S SW W NW

TEMPERATURE

MAX./MIN. _____ °F/°C

PRECIPITATION

CONDITIONS

WIND

N NE E SE S SW W NW

TEMPERATURE

MAX./MIN. _____ °F/°C

PRECIPITATION

CONDITIONS

WIND

N NE E SE S SW W NW

Week of _____ *to* _____
(month, day)   (month, day)

THURSDAY	FRIDAY	SATURDAY	SUNDAY

TEMPERATURE	TEMPERATURE	TEMPERATURE	TEMPERATURE
MAX./MIN. _____ °F/°C	MAX./MIN. _____ °F/°C	MAX./MIN. _____ °F/°C	MAX./MIN. _____ °F/°C
PRECIPITATION	PRECIPITATION	PRECIPITATION	PRECIPITATION
CONDITIONS	CONDITIONS	CONDITIONS	CONDITIONS
WIND	WIND	WIND	WIND
N NE E SE S SW W NW	N NE E SE S SW W NW	N NE E SE S SW W NW	N NE E SE S SW W NW

S U M M E R

MONDAY	TUESDAY	WEDNESDAY	THURSDAY

TEMPERATURE	TEMPERATURE	TEMPERATURE	TEMPERATURE
MAX./MIN. _____ °F/°C	MAX./MIN. _____ °F/°C	MAX./MIN. _____ °F/°C	MAX./MIN. _____ °F/°C

PRECIPITATION · PRECIPITATION · PRECIPITATION · PRECIPITATION

CONDITIONS · CONDITIONS · CONDITIONS · CONDITIONS

WIND · WIND · WIND · WIND

N NE E SE S SW W NW N NE E SE S SW W NW N NE E SE S SW W NW N NE E SE S SW W NW

Week of _____ to _____
(month, day)   *(month, day)*

FRIDAY	SATURDAY	SUNDAY

TEMPERATURE

MAX./MIN. _____ °F/°C

PRECIPITATION

CONDITIONS

WIND

N NE E SE S SW W NW

TEMPERATURE

MAX./MIN. _____ °F/°C

PRECIPITATION

CONDITIONS

WIND

N NE E SE S SW W NW

TEMPERATURE

MAX./MIN. _____ °F/°C

PRECIPITATION

CONDITIONS

WIND

N NE E SE S SW W NW

SUMMER

MONDAY	TUESDAY	WEDNESDAY

Water is one of the basics of life. Learn to harness and conserve this valuable resource. Get in the habit of watering early in the morning. This means more water for the plants and less wasted by the heat of the day.

TEMPERATURE	TEMPERATURE	TEMPERATURE
MAX./MIN. _____ °F/°C	MAX./MIN. _____ °F/°C	MAX./MIN. _____ °F/°C
PRECIPITATION	PRECIPITATION	PRECIPITATION
CONDITIONS	CONDITIONS	CONDITIONS
WIND	WIND	WIND
N NE E SE S SW W NW	N NE E SE S SW W NW	N NE E SE S SW W NW

Week of _____ *to* _____
(month, day)   (month, day)

THURSDAY	FRIDAY	SATURDAY	SUNDAY

TEMPERATURE

MAX./MIN. _____ °F/°C

PRECIPITATION

CONDITIONS

WIND

N NE E SE S SW W NW

TEMPERATURE

MAX./MIN. _____ °F/°C

PRECIPITATION

CONDITIONS

WIND

N NE E SE S SW W NW

TEMPERATURE

MAX./MIN. _____ °F/°C

PRECIPITATION

CONDITIONS

WIND

N NE E SE S SW W NW

TEMPERATURE

MAX./MIN. _____ °F/°C

PRECIPITATION

CONDITIONS

WIND

N NE E SE S SW W NW

SUMMER

MONDAY	TUESDAY	WEDNESDAY	THURSDAY

TEMPERATURE

MAX./MIN. _____°F/°C

PRECIPITATION

CONDITIONS

WIND

N NE E SE S SW W NW

TEMPERATURE

MAX./MIN. _____°F/°C

PRECIPITATION

CONDITIONS

WIND

N NE E SE S SW W NW

TEMPERATURE

MAX./MIN. _____°F/°C

PRECIPITATION

CONDITIONS

WIND

N NE E SE S SW W NW

TEMPERATURE

MAX./MIN. _____°F/°C

PRECIPITATION

CONDITIONS

WIND

N NE E SE S SW W NW

Week of _____ *to* _____
(month, day)   (month, day)

FRIDAY	SATURDAY	SUNDAY

TEMPERATURE

MAX./MIN. _____ °F/°C

PRECIPITATION

CONDITIONS

WIND

N NE E SE S SW W NW

TEMPERATURE

MAX./MIN. _____ °F/°C

PRECIPITATION

CONDITIONS

WIND

N NE E SE S SW W NW

TEMPERATURE

MAX./MIN. _____ °F/°C

PRECIPITATION

CONDITIONS

WIND

N NE E SE S SW W NW

"I think it pisses God off if you walk by the color purple in a field somewhere and don't notice it."
ALICE WALKER

SUMMER

MONDAY	TUESDAY	WEDNESDAY

Take time to enjoy your garden and the work you've contributed. Step back, relax, and plop down in a chair to just observe for a spell. Smell the ripening tomatoes cooking in the sun on vines you have nurtured.

TEMPERATURE	TEMPERATURE	TEMPERATURE
MAX./MIN. _____ °F/°C	MAX./MIN. _____ °F/°C	MAX./MIN. _____ °F/°C
PRECIPITATION	PRECIPITATION	PRECIPITATION
CONDITIONS	CONDITIONS	CONDITIONS
WIND	WIND	WIND
N NE E SE S SW W NW	N NE E SE S SW W NW	N NE E SE S SW W NW

Week of _____ *to* _____
(month, day)   (month, day)

THURSDAY	FRIDAY	SATURDAY	SUNDAY

TEMPERATURE

MAX./MIN. _____ °F/°C

PRECIPITATION

CONDITIONS

WIND

N NE E SE S SW W NW

TEMPERATURE

MAX./MIN. _____ °F/°C

PRECIPITATION

CONDITIONS

WIND

N NE E SE S SW W NW

TEMPERATURE

MAX./MIN. _____ °F/°C

PRECIPITATION

CONDITIONS

WIND

N NE E SE S SW W NW

TEMPERATURE

MAX./MIN. _____ °F/°C

PRECIPITATION

CONDITIONS

WIND

N NE E SE S SW W NW

SUMMER

MONDAY	TUESDAY	WEDNESDAY	THURSDAY

TEMPERATURE

MAX./MIN. _____ °F/°C

PRECIPITATION

CONDITIONS

WIND

N NE E SE S SW W NW

TEMPERATURE

MAX./MIN. _____ °F/°C

PRECIPITATION

CONDITIONS

WIND

N NE E SE S SW W NW

TEMPERATURE

MAX./MIN. _____ °F/°C

PRECIPITATION

CONDITIONS

WIND

N NE E SE S SW W NW

TEMPERATURE

MAX./MIN. _____ °F/°C

PRECIPITATION

CONDITIONS

WIND

N NE E SE S SW W NW

FRIDAY	SATURDAY	SUNDAY

"*I came to love my rows,
my beans,
Though so many more than
I wanted.
They attached me to the
earth, and so I got strength
like Antaeus.*"

HENRY DAVID THOREAU

TEMPERATURE	TEMPERATURE	TEMPERATURE
MAX./MIN. _____ °F/°C	MAX./MIN. _____ °F/°C	MAX./MIN. _____ °F/°C
PRECIPITATION	PRECIPITATION	PRECIPITATION
CONDITIONS	CONDITIONS	CONDITIONS
WIND	WIND	WIND
N NE E SE S SW W NW	N NE E SE S SW W NW	N NE E SE S SW W NW

SUMMER

MONDAY	TUESDAY	WEDNESDAY

TEMPERATURE	TEMPERATURE	TEMPERATURE
MAX./MIN. _____ °F/°C	MAX./MIN. _____ °F/°C	MAX./MIN. _____ °F/°C
PRECIPITATION	PRECIPITATION	PRECIPITATION
CONDITIONS	CONDITIONS	CONDITIONS
WIND	WIND	WIND
N NE E SE S SW W NW	N NE E SE S SW W NW	N NE E SE S SW W NW

THURSDAY	FRIDAY	SATURDAY	SUNDAY

THURSDAY

TEMPERATURE

MAX./MIN. _____ °F/°C

PRECIPITATION

CONDITIONS

WIND

N NE E SE S SW W NW

FRIDAY

TEMPERATURE

MAX./MIN. _____ °F/°C

PRECIPITATION

CONDITIONS

WIND

N NE E SE S SW W NW

SATURDAY

TEMPERATURE

MAX./MIN. _____ °F/°C

PRECIPITATION

CONDITIONS

WIND

N NE E SE S SW W NW

SUNDAY

TEMPERATURE

MAX./MIN. _____ °F/°C

PRECIPITATION

CONDITIONS

WIND

N NE E SE S SW W NW

SUMMER

MONDAY	TUESDAY	WEDNESDAY	THURSDAY

TEMPERATURE

MAX./MIN. _____ °F/°C

PRECIPITATION

CONDITIONS

WIND

N NE E SE S SW W NW

TEMPERATURE

MAX./MIN. _____ °F/°C

PRECIPITATION

CONDITIONS

WIND

N NE E SE S SW W NW

TEMPERATURE

MAX./MIN. _____ °F/°C

PRECIPITATION

CONDITIONS

WIND

N NE E SE S SW W NW

TEMPERATURE

MAX./MIN. _____ °F/°C

PRECIPITATION

CONDITIONS

WIND

N NE E SE S SW W NW

Week of _____ *to* _____
(month, day)   (month, day)

FRIDAY	SATURDAY	SUNDAY

TEMPERATURE

MAX./MIN. _____ °F/°C

PRECIPITATION

CONDITIONS

WIND

N NE E SE S SW W NW

TEMPERATURE

MAX./MIN. _____ °F/°C

PRECIPITATION

CONDITIONS

WIND

N NE E SE S SW W NW

TEMPERATURE

MAX./MIN. _____ °F/°C

PRECIPITATION

CONDITIONS

WIND

N NE E SE S SW W NW

SUMMER

MONDAY	TUESDAY	WEDNESDAY

Immortalize your best plants by taking seeds from them. Prepare them for drying and storing for next year's crop.

Put nitrogen back into the soil and keep it there with freshly planted cover crops.

TEMPERATURE	TEMPERATURE	TEMPERATURE
MAX./MIN. _____ °F/°C	MAX./MIN. _____ °F/°C	MAX./MIN. _____ °F/°C
PRECIPITATION	PRECIPITATION	PRECIPITATION
CONDITIONS	CONDITIONS	CONDITIONS
WIND	WIND	WIND
N NE E SE S SW W NW	N NE E SE S SW W NW	N NE E SE S SW W NW

Week of _____ *to* _____
(month, day)   (month, day)

THURSDAY	FRIDAY	SATURDAY	SUNDAY

TEMPERATURE

MAX./MIN. _____ °F/°C

PRECIPITATION

CONDITIONS

WIND

N NE E SE S SW W NW

TEMPERATURE

MAX./MIN. _____ °F/°C

PRECIPITATION

CONDITIONS

WIND

N NE E SE S SW W NW

TEMPERATURE

MAX./MIN. _____ °F/°C

PRECIPITATION

CONDITIONS

WIND

N NE E SE S SW W NW

TEMPERATURE

MAX./MIN. _____ °F/°C

PRECIPITATION

CONDITIONS

WIND

N NE E SE S SW W NW

AUTUMN

GARDEN

MONTHLY

NOTES

October

November

December

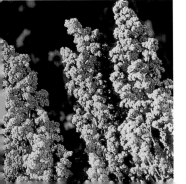

GARDENING

A U T U M N

MONDAY	TUESDAY	WEDNESDAY

Take time to reflect upon all that you have accomplished and witnessed in the cycle of life.

The cool ground is comfort for root vegetables, so harvest them as late in the season as possible.

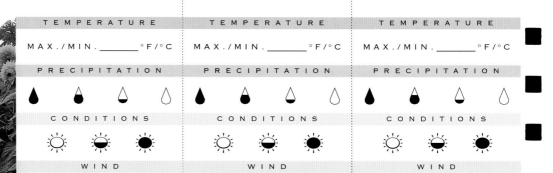

TEMPERATURE	TEMPERATURE	TEMPERATURE
MAX./MIN. _____ °F/°C	MAX./MIN. _____ °F/°C	MAX./MIN. _____ °F/°C
PRECIPITATION	PRECIPITATION	PRECIPITATION
CONDITIONS	CONDITIONS	CONDITIONS
WIND	WIND	WIND
N NE E SE S SW W NW	N NE E SE S SW W NW	N NE E SE S SW W NW

THURSDAY	FRIDAY	SATURDAY	SUNDAY

TEMPERATURE	TEMPERATURE	TEMPERATURE	TEMPERATURE
MAX./MIN. _____ °F/°C	MAX./MIN. _____ °F/°C	MAX./MIN. _____ °F/°C	MAX./MIN. _____ °F/°C
PRECIPITATION	PRECIPITATION	PRECIPITATION	PRECIPITATION
CONDITIONS	CONDITIONS	CONDITIONS	CONDITIONS
WIND	WIND	WIND	WIND
N NE E SE S SW W NW	N NE E SE S SW W NW	N NE E SE S SW W NW	N NE E SE S SW W NW

AUTUMN

MONDAY	TUESDAY	WEDNESDAY	THURSDAY

TEMPERATURE | TEMPERATURE | TEMPERATURE | TEMPERATURE

MAX./MIN. _____ °F/°C | MAX./MIN. _____ °F/°C | MAX./MIN. _____ °F/°C | MAX./MIN. _____ °F/°C

PRECIPITATION | PRECIPITATION | PRECIPITATION | PRECIPITATION

CONDITIONS | CONDITIONS | CONDITIONS | CONDITIONS

WIND | WIND | WIND | WIND

N NE E SE S SW W NW | N NE E SE S SW W NW | N NE E SE S SW W NW | N NE E SE S SW W NW

Week of _____ *to* _____
(month, day)   (month, day)

FRIDAY	SATURDAY	SUNDAY

TEMPERATURE

MAX./MIN. _____ °F/°C

TEMPERATURE

MAX./MIN. _____ °F/°C

TEMPERATURE

MAX./MIN. _____ °F/°C

PRECIPITATION

PRECIPITATION

PRECIPITATION

CONDITIONS

CONDITIONS

CONDITIONS

WIND

N NE E SE S SW W NW

WIND

N NE E SE S SW W NW

WIND

N NE E SE S SW W NW

"To sleep in curved furrows
Blanketed by the moon
We are jealous of the crops."
S.E. GLASS

AUTUMN

MONDAY	TUESDAY	WEDNESDAY

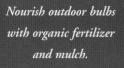

Collect leaves for the compost pile. Don't feel like raking? Simply mow over them and leave them as composting mulch for your lawn.

Nourish outdoor bulbs with organic fertilizer and mulch.

TEMPERATURE	TEMPERATURE	TEMPERATURE
MAX./MIN. _____ °F/°C	MAX./MIN. _____ °F/°C	MAX./MIN. _____ °F/°C
PRECIPITATION	PRECIPITATION	PRECIPITATION
CONDITIONS	CONDITIONS	CONDITIONS
WIND	WIND	WIND
N NE E SE S SW W NW	N NE E SE S SW W NW	N NE E SE S SW W NW

Week of _____ *to* _____
        (month, day)   (month, day)

THURSDAY	FRIDAY	SATURDAY	SUNDAY

TEMPERATURE	TEMPERATURE	TEMPERATURE	TEMPERATURE
MAX./MIN. _____ °F/°C	MAX./MIN. _____ °F/°C	MAX./MIN. _____ °F/°C	MAX./MIN. _____ °F/°C
PRECIPITATION	PRECIPITATION	PRECIPITATION	PRECIPITATION
CONDITIONS	CONDITIONS	CONDITIONS	CONDITIONS
WIND	WIND	WIND	WIND
N NE E SE S SW W NW	N NE E SE S SW W NW	N NE E SE S SW W NW	N NE E SE S SW W NW

AUTUMN

MONDAY	TUESDAY	WEDNESDAY	THURSDAY

TEMPERATURE

MAX./MIN. _____ °F/°C

PRECIPITATION

CONDITIONS

WIND

N NE E SE S SW W NW

TEMPERATURE

MAX./MIN. _____ °F/°C

PRECIPITATION

CONDITIONS

WIND

N NE E SE S SW W NW

TEMPERATURE

MAX./MIN. _____ °F/°C

PRECIPITATION

CONDITIONS

WIND

N NE E SE S SW W NW

TEMPERATURE

MAX./MIN. _____ °F/°C

PRECIPITATION

CONDITIONS

WIND

N NE E SE S SW W NW

FRIDAY	SATURDAY	SUNDAY

> "Nature is just enough;
> but men and women must
> comprehend and accept her
> suggestions."
> ANTOINETTE BROWN
> BLACKWELL

TEMPERATURE	TEMPERATURE	TEMPERATURE
MAX./MIN. _____ °F/°C	MAX./MIN. _____ °F/°C	MAX./MIN. _____ °F/°C
PRECIPITATION	PRECIPITATION	PRECIPITATION
CONDITIONS	CONDITIONS	CONDITIONS
WIND	WIND	WIND
N NE E SE S SW W NW	N NE E SE S SW W NW	N NE E SE S SW W NW

AUTUMN

MONDAY	TUESDAY	WEDNESDAY

As this season begins to
wind down, get a jump on
next year's.

Now is a good time to
dig, compost, and mulch
your soil. This will prepare
for the spring and protect it
for the winter.

TEMPERATURE	TEMPERATURE	TEMPERATURE
MAX./MIN. _____ °F/°C	MAX./MIN. _____ °F/°C	MAX./MIN. _____ °F/°C
PRECIPITATION	PRECIPITATION	PRECIPITATION
CONDITIONS	CONDITIONS	CONDITIONS
WIND	WIND	WIND
N NE E SE S SW W NW	N NE E SE S SW W NW	N NE E SE S SW W NW

Week of _____ *to* _____
(month, day)   (month, day)

THURSDAY	FRIDAY	SATURDAY	SUNDAY

TEMPERATURE	TEMPERATURE	TEMPERATURE	TEMPERATURE
MAX./MIN. _____ °F/°C	MAX./MIN. _____ °F/°C	MAX./MIN. _____ °F/°C	MAX./MIN. _____ °F/°C

PRECIPITATION   PRECIPITATION   PRECIPITATION   PRECIPITATION

CONDITIONS   CONDITIONS   CONDITIONS   CONDITIONS

WIND   WIND   WIND   WIND

N NE E SE S SW W NW   N NE E SE S SW W NW   N NE E SE S SW W NW   N NE E SE S SW W NW

AUTUMN

MONDAY	TUESDAY	WEDNESDAY	THURSDAY

TEMPERATURE	TEMPERATURE	TEMPERATURE	TEMPERATURE
MAX./MIN. _____ °F/°C	MAX./MIN. _____ °F/°C	MAX./MIN. _____ °F/°C	MAX./MIN. _____ °F/°C
PRECIPITATION	PRECIPITATION	PRECIPITATION	PRECIPITATION
CONDITIONS	CONDITIONS	CONDITIONS	CONDITIONS
WIND	WIND	WIND	WIND
N NE E SE S SW W NW	N NE E SE S SW W NW	N NE E SE S SW W NW	N NE E SE S SW W NW

Week of _____ *to* _____
                    (month, day)   (month, day)

FRIDAY	SATURDAY	SUNDAY

TEMPERATURE

MAX./MIN. _____ °F/°C

PRECIPITATION

CONDITIONS

WIND

N NE E SE S SW W NW

TEMPERATURE

MAX./MIN. _____ °F/°C

PRECIPITATION

CONDITIONS

WIND

N NE E SE S SW W NW

TEMPERATURE

MAX./MIN. _____ °F/°C

PRECIPITATION

CONDITIONS

WIND

N NE E SE S SW W NW

"Those who labor in the earth are the chosen people of God, if ever he had a chosen people."

THOMAS JEFFERSON

AUTUMN

MONDAY	TUESDAY	WEDNESDAY

*Clean tools and equipment
before storing, so they are
ready when you need them.
Remember to drain hoses
before coiling.*

TEMPERATURE

MAX./MIN. _____ °F/°C

PRECIPITATION

CONDITIONS

WIND

N NE E SE S SW W NW

TEMPERATURE

MAX./MIN. _____ °F/°C

PRECIPITATION

CONDITIONS

WIND

N NE E SE S SW W NW

TEMPERATURE

MAX./MIN. _____ °F/°C

PRECIPITATION

CONDITIONS

WIND

N NE E SE S SW W NW

Week of _____ *to* _____
(month, day)   (month, day)

THURSDAY	FRIDAY	SATURDAY	SUNDAY

TEMPERATURE

MAX./MIN. _____ °F/°C

PRECIPITATION

CONDITIONS

WIND

N NE E SE S SW W NW

TEMPERATURE

MAX./MIN. _____ °F/°C

PRECIPITATION

CONDITIONS

WIND

N NE E SE S SW W NW

TEMPERATURE

MAX./MIN. _____ °F/°C

PRECIPITATION

CONDITIONS

WIND

N NE E SE S SW W NW

TEMPERATURE

MAX./MIN. _____ °F/°C

PRECIPITATION

CONDITIONS

WIND

N NE E SE S SW W NW

AUTUMN

MONDAY	TUESDAY	WEDNESDAY	THURSDAY

TEMPERATURE

MAX./MIN. _____ °F/°C

PRECIPITATION

CONDITIONS

WIND

N NE E SE S SW W NW

TEMPERATURE

MAX./MIN. _____ °F/°C

PRECIPITATION

CONDITIONS

WIND

N NE E SE S SW W NW

TEMPERATURE

MAX./MIN. _____ °F/°C

PRECIPITATION

CONDITIONS

WIND

N NE E SE S SW W NW

TEMPERATURE

MAX./MIN. _____ °F/°C

PRECIPITATION

CONDITIONS

WIND

N NE E SE S SW W NW

Week of _____ *to* _____
(month, day)   (month, day)

FRIDAY	SATURDAY	SUNDAY

"Nature's silence is its
one remark, and every flake
of world
is a chip off that old mute
and immutable block."
ANNIE DILLARD

TEMPERATURE	TEMPERATURE	TEMPERATURE
MAX./MIN. _____ °F/°C	MAX./MIN. _____ °F/°C	MAX./MIN. _____ °F/°C
PRECIPITATION	PRECIPITATION	PRECIPITATION
CONDITIONS	CONDITIONS	CONDITIONS
WIND	WIND	WIND
N NE E SE S SW W NW	N NE E SE S SW W NW	N NE E SE S SW W NW

AUTUMN

Read up on different plants and planting ideas and incorporate what you have learned into future endeavors.

Maintain cold weather cloches into the new year.

MONDAY	TUESDAY	WEDNESDAY

TEMPERATURE

MAX./MIN. _____ °F/°C

PRECIPITATION

CONDITIONS

WIND

N NE E SE S SW W NW

TEMPERATURE

MAX./MIN. _____ °F/°C

PRECIPITATION

CONDITIONS

WIND

N NE E SE S SW W NW

TEMPERATURE

MAX./MIN. _____ °F/°C

PRECIPITATION

CONDITIONS

WIND

N NE E SE S SW W NW

Week of _____ *to* _____
(month, day)   (month, day)

THURSDAY	FRIDAY	SATURDAY	SUNDAY

TEMPERATURE	TEMPERATURE	TEMPERATURE	TEMPERATURE
MAX./MIN. _____ °F/°C	MAX./MIN. _____ °F/°C	MAX./MIN. _____ °F/°C	MAX./MIN. _____ °F/°C
PRECIPITATION	PRECIPITATION	PRECIPITATION	PRECIPITATION
CONDITIONS	CONDITIONS	CONDITIONS	CONDITIONS
WIND	WIND	WIND	WIND
N NE E SE S SW W NW	N NE E SE S SW W NW	N NE E SE S SW W NW	N NE E SE S SW W NW

AUTUMN

MONDAY	TUESDAY	WEDNESDAY	THURSDAY

TEMPERATURE

MAX./MIN. _____ °F/°C

PRECIPITATION

CONDITIONS

WIND

N NE E SE S SW W NW

TEMPERATURE

MAX./MIN. _____ °F/°C

PRECIPITATION

CONDITIONS

WIND

N NE E SE S SW W NW

TEMPERATURE

MAX./MIN. _____ °F/°C

PRECIPITATION

CONDITIONS

WIND

N NE E SE S SW W NW

TEMPERATURE

MAX./MIN. _____ °F/°C

PRECIPITATION

CONDITIONS

WIND

N NE E SE S SW W NW

Week of _____ to _____
(month, day)   *(month, day)*

FRIDAY	SATURDAY	SUNDAY

"There is a wilder solitude
in winter
When every sense is pricked
alive and keen."
MAY SARTON

TEMPERATURE	TEMPERATURE	TEMPERATURE
MAX./MIN. _____ °F/°C	MAX./MIN. _____ °F/°C	MAX./MIN. _____ °F/°C
PRECIPITATION	PRECIPITATION	PRECIPITATION
CONDITIONS	CONDITIONS	CONDITIONS
WIND	WIND	WIND
N NE E SE S SW W NW	N NE E SE S SW W NW	N NE E SE S SW W NW

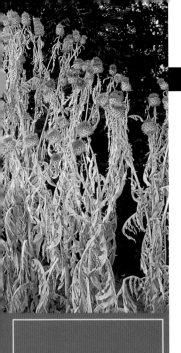

AUTUMN

MONDAY	TUESDAY	WEDNESDAY

Start thumbing through the seed catalogs and place orders for a new and even better garden. Treat your-self to needed garden tools during the holidays.

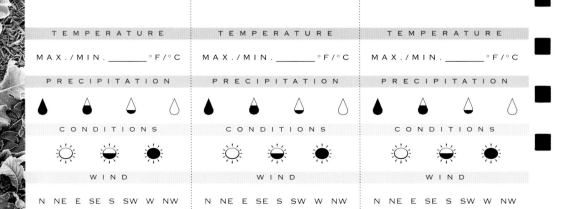

TEMPERATURE	TEMPERATURE	TEMPERATURE
MAX./MIN. _____ °F/°C	MAX./MIN. _____ °F/°C	MAX./MIN. _____ °F/°C
PRECIPITATION	PRECIPITATION	PRECIPITATION
CONDITIONS	CONDITIONS	CONDITIONS
WIND	WIND	WIND
N NE E SE S SW W NW	N NE E SE S SW W NW	N NE E SE S SW W NW

Week of _____ *to* _____
(month, day)   *(month, day)*

THURSDAY	FRIDAY	SATURDAY	SUNDAY

TEMPERATURE

MAX./MIN. _____ °F/°C

PRECIPITATION

CONDITIONS

WIND

N NE E SE S SW W NW

TEMPERATURE

MAX./MIN. _____ °F/°C

PRECIPITATION

CONDITIONS

WIND

N NE E SE S SW W NW

TEMPERATURE

MAX./MIN. _____ °F/°C

PRECIPITATION

CONDITIONS

WIND

N NE E SE S SW W NW

TEMPERATURE

MAX./MIN. _____ °F/°C

PRECIPITATION

CONDITIONS

WIND

N NE E SE S SW W NW

AUTUMN

MONDAY	TUESDAY	WEDNESDAY	THURSDAY

TEMPERATURE

MAX./MIN. _____ °F/°C

PRECIPITATION

CONDITIONS

WIND

N NE E SE S SW W NW

TEMPERATURE

MAX./MIN. _____ °F/°C

PRECIPITATION

CONDITIONS

WIND

N NE E SE S SW W NW

TEMPERATURE

MAX./MIN. _____ °F/°C

PRECIPITATION

CONDITIONS

WIND

N NE E SE S SW W NW

TEMPERATURE

MAX./MIN. _____ °F/°C

PRECIPITATION

CONDITIONS

WIND

N NE E SE S SW W NW

Week of _____ *to* _____
(month, day)   (month, day)

FRIDAY	SATURDAY	SUNDAY

TEMPERATURE

MAX./MIN. _____ °F/°C

PRECIPITATION

CONDITIONS

WIND

N NE E SE S SW W NW

TEMPERATURE

MAX./MIN. _____ °F/°C

PRECIPITATION

CONDITIONS

WIND

N NE E SE S SW W NW

TEMPERATURE

MAX./MIN. _____ °F/°C

PRECIPITATION

CONDITIONS

WIND

N NE E SE S SW W NW

AUTUMN

A time for reflecting on this year's successes and failures in the garden—and on the cycle of nature you have observed.

TEMPERATURE

MAX./MIN. _____ °F/°C

PRECIPITATION

CONDITIONS

WIND

N NE E SE S SW W NW

TEMPERATURE

MAX./MIN. _____ °F/°C

PRECIPITATION

CONDITIONS

WIND

N NE E SE S SW W NW

TEMPERATURE

MAX./MIN. _____ °F/°C

PRECIPITATION

CONDITIONS

WIND

N NE E SE S SW W NW

Week of _____ *to* _____
(month, day)   *(month, day)*

THURSDAY	FRIDAY	SATURDAY	SUNDAY

TEMPERATURE

MAX./MIN. _____ °F/°C

PRECIPITATION

CONDITIONS

WIND

N NE E SE S SW W NW

TEMPERATURE

MAX./MIN. _____ °F/°C

PRECIPITATION

CONDITIONS

WIND

N NE E SE S SW W NW

TEMPERATURE

MAX./MIN. _____ °F/°C

PRECIPITATION

CONDITIONS

WIND

N NE E SE S SW W NW

TEMPERATURE

MAX./MIN. _____ °F/°C

PRECIPITATION

CONDITIONS

WIND

N NE E SE S SW W NW

AUTUMN

MONDAY	TUESDAY	WEDNESDAY	THURSDAY

TEMPERATURE

MAX./MIN. _____ °F/°C

PRECIPITATION

CONDITIONS

WIND

N NE E SE S SW W NW

TEMPERATURE

MAX./MIN. _____ °F/°C

PRECIPITATION

CONDITIONS

WIND

N NE E SE S SW W NW

TEMPERATURE

MAX./MIN. _____ °F/°C

PRECIPITATION

CONDITIONS

WIND

N NE E SE S SW W NW

TEMPERATURE

MAX./MIN. _____ °F/°C

PRECIPITATION

CONDITIONS

WIND

N NE E SE S SW W NW

Week of _____ *to* _____
(month, day)   (month, day)

FRIDAY	SATURDAY	SUNDAY

"Winter is an abstract season; it is low on colours . . . and big on the imperatives of cold and brief daylight . . . beauty at low temperatures is beauty."
JOSEPH BRODSKY

TEMPERATURE

MAX./MIN. _____ °F/°C

PRECIPITATION

CONDITIONS

WIND

N NE E SE S SW W NW

TEMPERATURE

MAX./MIN. _____ °F/°C

PRECIPITATION

CONDITIONS

WIND

N NE E SE S SW W NW

TEMPERATURE

MAX./MIN. _____ °F/°C

PRECIPITATION

CONDITIONS

WIND

N NE E SE S SW W NW

GARDENING

1. SEED COMPANIES

Seeds of Change
Certified Organic
PO Box 15700
Santa Fe, NM 87506-5700
Phone: (888) 762-7333 / *Fax:* (888) 329-4762
E-mail: gardener@seedsofchange.com
www.seedsofchange.com

Deep Diversity
A Planetary Gene Pool Resource
PO Box 15700
Santa Fe, NM 87506-5700
(Contact by mail only)

Abundant Life
PO Box 772
1029 Lawrence Street
Port Townsend, WA 98368
Phone: (360) 385-5660 / *Fax:* (360) 385-7455

Bountiful Gardens
18001 Shafer Ranch Road
Willits, CA 95490-9626
Phone: (707) 459-6410

Elixir Farm Botanicals
(Medicinal Plant Seeds)
Brixey, MO 65618
Phone: (417) 261-2393

Garden City Seeds
778 Hwy. 93N
Hamilton, MT 59840-9448
Phone: (406) 961-4837 / *Fax:* (406) 961-4877

J.L. Hudson, Seedsman
Star Route 2, Box 337
La Honda, CA 94929
(Contact by mail only)

Native Seeds/Search
526 North 4th Avenue
Tucson, AZ 85705
Phone: (520) 622-5561 / *Fax:* (520) 622-5591

Prairie Moon Nursery
Route 3, Box 163
Winona, MN 55987-9515
Phone: (507) 452-1362 / *Fax:* (507) 454-5238

Seed Savers Exchange
3076 North Winn Road
Decorah, IA 52101
Phone: (319) 382-5990

Synergy Seeds
PO Box 787
Somes Bar, CA 95568
Phone: (916) 321-3769

2. RARE FRUIT TREES

Exotica Rare Fruit Nursery
PO Box 160
Vista, CA 92085
Phone: (619) 724-9093

Sonoma Antique Apple Nursery
4395 Westside Road
Healdsburg, CA 95448
Phone: (707) 433-6420

Southmeadow Fruit Farms
Box SM
Lakeside, MI 49116
Phone: (616) 469-2865

RESOURCES

3. INTERESTING TREES & PLANTS

Forest Farm
990 Tetherow Road
Williams, OR 97544-9599
Phone: (541) 846-7269 / *Fax:* (541) 846-6963

Glasshouse Works
Church Street
Stewart, OH 45778-0097
Phone: (614) 662-2142

Logee's Greenhouses
141 North Street
Danielson, CT 06239
Phone: (203) 774-8038 / *Fax:* (203) 774-9932

Mesa Garden
PO Box 72
Belen, NM 87002
Phone: (505) 864-3131 / *Fax:* (505) 864-3124

Northern Groves Bamboo
PO Box 86291
Portland, OR 97286-0291
Phone: (503) 774-6353

Plants of the Southwest
Agua Fria, Rt. 6, Box 11A
Santa Fe, NM 87505
Phone: (505) 471-2212

Rare Conifer Nursery
PO Box 100
Potter Valley, CA 95469
Fax: (707) 462-9536
(Contact by mail or fax only)

4. ORGANIZATIONS

The Bio-Dynamic Farming and Gardening Association, Inc.
Bldg. 1002B, Thoreau Center,
The Presidio
PO Box 29135
San Francisco, CA 94129-0135
Phone: (415) 561-7797 / *Fax:* (415) 561-7796
E-mail: Biodynamic@aol.com

Ecology Action
Sustainable Biointensive Mini-Farming
5798 Ridgewood Road
Willits, CA 95490
Phone: (707) 459-0150 / *Fax:* (707) 459-5409

The Land Institute
2440 Water Well Road
Salina, KS 67401
Phone: (913) 823-5376 / *Fax:* (913) 823-8728

The Permaculture Institute
PO Box 3702
Pojoaque, NM 87501
(Contact by mail only)

5. OTHER
There are a large number of societies dedicated to almost every type of popular plant or tree. For information and further sources, contact your local botanical garden or agricultural extension agent. Alternatively, check the Internet.